From Broke To Bentley

My Journey To Success

Book 1

JAMAAL ALI

Dedication

This book is dedicated to none other than my lovely mother, Mary Lee Epps. I am because you are. In every way, you're an integral part of me, all I am, and all I'll ever be. Your never wavering love and support has kept me in the game of life. You are my inspiration and my rock. You taught me well and I owe everything I am to you. I pray that I make you proud

.

CONTENTS

Acknowledgments

To Lisa Nichols, creator of "Motivating the Masses" and "Speak and Write to Make Millions." To Steve, Kathy and Amber Kidd of "KIDD Marketing." Without you all, this would have never happened. Thanks for serving from your overflow. Willing you Peace, Love and Prosperity. We are forever joined at the hip and in the heart.

Finally, to my sister Tafi who invested and enabled me to start this journey towards greatness. Thank you for believing in me, thank you for saying yes. Though you're my little sister, when I grow up,
I want to be just like you. Love you girl..

Jamaal Ali

Foreward

It's unbelievable when you decide to press that reset button, the great things that can happen. I met Jamaal a few years ago at Motivating The Masses in Atlanta, the first thing that caught my eyes were his attire, he was impeccably dressed and his carriage was amazing. I've been in the fashion industry for two decades so when people stand out I notice. We had the opportunity to interact over the three days and he was super inspiring, we kept in touch ever since but last year I really got a better picture of who Jamaal Abdul-Ali really is. I attended Girl Go Be Great in Atlanta again and I was late for the afternoon session so I decided to slip in at the back to listen to the speaker and the person was the only male speaker at a women's conference and he was tall dark and handsome. I was totally captivated by his presentation and so were the other women. It was evident how much Les Brown had influenced his life, he used a lot of Les quotes which resonated with me because Les Brown is one of my mentors. It was an honour to introduce Jamaal and Les because they have so much in common and they hit it off immediately just like I thought they would. Every life has a story and I always knew that Jamaal's story would make an incredible book, from a star athlete to a drug addict must have taken him deep into that valley most people never come out of. To bounce back from 20 years of drug and alcohol abuse to the man he is today is commendable, that world is so hard it's like coming from hell to heaven, it's hard to believe that the Jamaal that I know today disrespected women in the past but that is what the dark side does to you. I strongly believe that God had a special purpose for my friend's life because he has had so many near death experiences. I feel his hurt as he reveal to us his authentic self and I also feel the love, commitment, celebration dedication, determination, resilience, focus, and the thirst to inspire and motivate the world. I'm honoured to be contributing to this best seller and I recommend that you get a cup of coffee, tea or a glass of wine and make yourself comfortable as you're about to go deep into the life of friend and brother JAMAAL ABDUL ALI.

Dr Sonia Noel
International Fashion Designers/Philanthropist

The Early Years…Zone 15

I remember it like it was yesterday. 1968 Lincoln Heights, Ohio, also known as Zone 15, living on Jackson Street, 1441 to be precise…After playing outside all day as was customary in those days, it was finally time to come inside, settle down and eventually go to bed. Still full of energy, I wasn't quite ready to settle down. Being an only child and not having another sibling to chop it up with, I had to find other ways to entertain myself. I took a liking to reading at an early age and eventually picked up a National Enquirer tabloid lying around. I thumbed through and read a few of the sensational stories of the day when I eventually landed in the classified section in the back of the magazine. It seemed like it was always something outrageous to buy or sell back there. I ran across an ad that really changed my thinking forever, seriously. Again, this moment has stuck in my memory so clearly.

The article featured a gentleman by the name of Mark O'Haroldson, a Real Estate Tycoon. He boasted of how you become a millionaire investing in Real Estate. That didn't excite me as much as the big house and fancy sports cars in the back ground. I thought he must know what he's talking about and I have to find out. There was a catch, there was a cost associated with buying the program and following Mark into the land of milk and honey. And, there was slight issue, I was only 12 years old and, well, I couldn't afford it. I mean, I could have, but it would have taken many, many months of saving my allowance. As they say, timing is everything in life. For me, it was a time of sowing, and a seed was planted. Although it took a really long time, but eventually it blossomed.

That ad and the possibility it represented to live life on a totally different level had a tremendous impact on me and my psyche. So much so that 50 years later, in 2018, it's still in my memory and I'm sharing it with you.

Unfortunately for me, there was nothing or no one in my hood that even came close to what Mr. O'Haroldson was sharing as his reality and it would be years before I would actually see with my own eyes any semblance of that kind of lifestyle. In a tabloid, really, how much of that stuff is actually real. At 12 years old, I had no idea, but there was something inside of me that said, what if, something said it's possible or Mr. O wouldn't be talking about, right. I was so naive or was I? Hell no, it was at that moment that the millionaire inside of me was born.

Reality has a cruel and unusual way of knocking you upside the head and reminding you to look around, your current situation is real. You see, in 1968, it was just my mom and I and she only made $1.35 an hour bringing home $54.00 a week and $216.00 a month...Before taxes...

I didn't know we were poor at the time because most other folks around us were kind of in the same boat, if you know what I mean. Some had a little more, while some a little less. It was pretty normal for your mom to say, son, go next door to Ms Blackwell's and tell her to send me a cup of sugar, some butter or hell even a couple slices of bread. Still, there was something special about those days. I miss those days, do you? We didn't have much, but at least I could dream and I did dream. One day, I'm gonna have my big house, my fancy cars and travel the world, just like Mr O'Haroldson

I was a smart kid and a great student but very naive and I had no idea what I wanted to do with my life. It's funny though, even at that age I knew I didn't want to work for anyone, that I was sure about. The one thing that I had going for me that was special is that I was a helluva athlete. Basketball, Football and Baseball. Because I was always the fastest or at least one of the fastest guys on any team I've played on, I was never on the track team. My thinking was since I'm already faster than everyone, why should I do that? Man, was my thinking flawed. It was definitely a missed opportunity. But hey, you don't know what you don't know. To be honest, I had the skillset that if polished enough, focused and committed enough I could have gone pro in any sport. Example, I'm having dinner with one of my childhood friends and High School Basketball teammates in 2016 when he leans over to his wife and says, "This is one of the guys I told you should have made the NBA"...To hear that from him was very humbling. He lives in Oklahoma, I'm in Atlanta and we see each other every five years at the class reunion. So at some point he's having a conversation with his wife about me having the ability to make it to the NBA. It was a beautiful thing because I never knew he felt that way about me and my game. And, guess what, that's not the only time I've heard that from my friends. Yes, your boy had game, what I lacked was a consistent focus, discipline and commitment. Still, I did very well as a collegiate player where I played Football as well. They say hindsight is 20/20 and it's hard to argue with that. Looking back, I had much more going for me than I realized. In fact, looking back as a well-rounded, experienced mature young man, I would say I had all I needed to be successful in life.

....

Left Turn

I didn't see it at the time, but I had such a wonderful, promising, sky's the limit kind of life ahead of me. I had it all, intelligent, witty, snappy dresser, charismatic, voted most likely to succeed, magnificent mom, had the prettiest girl in high school, (awww) I can still see her face, star athlete, I was rolling. Went on to play college football and basketball, even had a couple of professional football tryouts. Destined for stardom, destined for greatness, life was good. Then...it all came tumbling down. Instead of becoming a star athlete, I became a star drug addict, when I say star I mean star, I was good at it, you see how you do anything is how you do everything. Somehow, I took a left turn and went on a twenty-year detour. Twenty years of drugs, alcohol, wine, women and song. You name the drug, I probably did it. Self-inflicted, self-induced misery and failure. Twenty years of, as the old folks say, just acting a darn fool...Now, you can replace the word darn with that other word that starts with a D, how many know what I'm talking about? Now, this was a very deep dark and troubling time in my life that's very difficult and very, very embarrassing for me to share, but I have to be authentic, I have to be transparent for that experience is a couple of chapters in the book of my life.

There's a high probability that many of you reading this have been affected either directly or indirectly. A father, uncle, brother, nephew, cousin, friend or friend of a friend. You know some male or female that was extremely talented, had everything going for them whose life was decimated by drugs.

I got to be real raw here and keep it 100 as they say. I've snorted heroin as well as cocaine and also freebased cocaine. I've smoked crack, marijuana and cigarettes sometimes all in the same setting. I've done all kinds of pills, uppers, downers, inners and outers. I've also sold the aforementioned drugs and often times became my own best customer. I've bought and sold women. I know, Jamaal, how could you? Listen, trust me when I say I am ashamed, embarrassed and truly sorry. I'm sorry for all the negative energy I released into the universe. I'm sorry for any and all pain I may have caused anyone along the way. Since most of those pains were self-inflicted, I say I'm sorry to myself. The drug world is a deep, dark, depressing, disgusting and unforgiving place. It's HELL.

I've been in places copping dope where everyone had a gun in their hands but me. Any crazy movements that even resemble possible trouble, and bang bang you're dead. But who really cares, just another black man murdered in a drug deal gone bad. I get it, no sympathy, after all, you put yourself in that position, that environment. You should've known better. Yes, I should have. Sounds real good in a book but in the real world it happens every day. I mean, no one sets out to be addicted to drugs, at least I didn't.

On two distinct occasions, I thought I was gonna OD. Once while freebasing cocaine and the other while smoking crack. I was so high, my heart racing so fast, so much pressure it felt as if my heart was gonna explode and burst out of my chest. I remember thinking, oh no, not a heart attack; please God, don't let me go out like this. What will they say about me, I have a beautiful reputation to uphold, how will my mother handle this? Not only has she lost her first child and only son, but I have also brought shame to her legacy and the family name. Not good Jamaal. Please God, don't let me go out like this. I promise, if you'll let me come down this time, if I can get back to normal I'll never do it again. I don't know how many times I told that lie over 20 years. I've been drunk on my ass and passed out more than a few times as well. Sad, sad story.

....

"Turn right and go straight" Jamaal Ali

....

The Ride

I have a lot of wild almost unbelievable yet true stories I could share, but this one takes the cake.

It was the summer of 1978, Spokane Washington, city of my discharge from the Air Force. Yes, yours truly served his country, thank you very much. Hanging out in the park in the summer with friends and or family is as American as apple pie. It was a beautiful almost magical day, so pretty, so clear, sun shining so bright. There is a short window for this kind of weather in Spokane, so when it's like this, everyone and their grandma is out. We were enjoying the typical out in the park festivities from flag football, frisbee, horseshoes, pets running around, music blaring, beer, booze, wine and lots of pot.

Trust me when I tell you the pot in those days was the best. Some of you old heads know what I'm talking about eh? I had a bad ass motorcycle, a 1972 Honda 750 cafe style former race bike converted to street legal. It was gorgeous and all the ladies wanted to ride and I had no problem with that. It's gonna be a great night cause I'm gonna hook up with one of these beauties for the night.

Well, that was my thinking, anyway. So much fun. After about six or seven hours of paradise in the park, people slowly but surely started to say their goodbyes. It was right at the time where sunlight ends and night begins. Early enough for folks to get home, rest a bit, get cleaned up and go out for the night. After all, it was Saturday night. I was a diehard and one of the last to leave. Once I got on my bike, I realized I had a slight problem. I was high as hell, intoxicated and had no business driving a car let alone riding a motorcycle. But hey, being the cowboy I am I saddled up and headed out. Very bad idea.

It didn't take long to realize I was in serious trouble. But when you're intoxicated, your thinking and rationale is impaired to the point of making stupid often times life changing fatal decisions. Now, it's fully night time and all the street light are on and all that jazz. I've only got about seven miles to get to the house so I figure I can make it. Just a couple of miles removed from the park and the unthinkable happens. As I'm sitting at the traffic light struggling to balance this bike, all of a sudden "bam" the bike falls over. Picture this now, I'm at the traffic light and I drop my bike, the light turns green and the people behind me are going ballistic screaming all sorts of profanities and everything else. But wait, it gets better, out of nowhere a cop pulls up behind me, he turns his lights on but never gets out his car. He acts a shield between me and the traffic. Meanwhile I'm just getting this heavy as bike upright and hop back on. Almost oblivious to the cop behind me, I pull off when the light turns green. He follows me acting sort of like an escort. I am doing really well, not really weaving and otherwise acting like I was drunk. After a mile or two while at another traffic light damn if I don't drop my bike again. Hilarious, I know, the cop is still behind, still has his light on and trying not to laugh himself stupid. Let me say this here and now, all cops ain't bad. This guy was a godsend, he was truly a guardian angel. I don't know if you know, but a motorcycle is really heavy when you're drunk and trying to get it upright after it's fallen over. I finally get back on and continue my journey my guardian angel not far behind, following not so close that it appeared he was pulling me over, but at the same time he wouldn't let anyone get in behind me.

All things considered I'm doing a damn good job, I mean, at least I'm not a threat to any oncoming traffic sense, I'm not weaving erratically and that sort of thing...I think if I was doing that the cop would have no choice but to pull me over and do his thing. Finally, I make it to my apartment complex. The cop follows me all the way in and stops about 20 feet from me and patiently watches as I park the bike and try to get off. BAM, I drop it again, right there in the parking space. By now the cop has seen enough. I can't describe the look of amazement or amusement on his face as he pulls away. I'm sure he's thinking nobody is going to believe this shit when I tell them. If he was smart he would only share this once in a lifetime encounter to a select few and in an intimate really close friend's type of environment. Listen, if it didn't actually happen to me I would have a hard time believing it myself.

Ok, since I'm home and in no need of hurrying to

pick this bike up one last time, I just sit there, in the dark, bike still running and I'm just there. I muster up enough strength to first get myself upright and then the daunting task of picking my baby up off the ground one last time. Wooo Hooo, I did it, got her up in position hit the kill switch and make it to the front door. I never made it inside, passed out right there. When I finally come to consciousness the next day, I realize I was lying in the bed, my girlfriend looking at me like I was her 5-year-old son or something. You know, that look you get when you have screwed up. She was so humble, so sweet, so understanding and so cool. In her loving voice, she said, "I came home and found you passed out in front of the door, don't ever scare me like that again. I thought you were dead. Do you know you wet your pants?" I felt like a 5-year-old, except I was a grown ass man and I don't know what the word is but I was ten times more than embarrassed. Just downright stupid, if I must say to myself.

I'm sharing all this with you to highlight a very important point. And that is, I'm very, very fortunate to be alive, fortunate to be sane enough, coherent enough, open and vulnerable enough to share this part of my life with you in a book form. You could not have told me at the age of 10 that I would enter into a world of drugs and remain there for 20 years. Not me, not the shy little kid with the big smile and humble demeanor. No way, it's just not consistent with my character. It doesn't seem real, it doesn't seem fair, why me. Why, why, why me? Though I've been totally clean for over 25 years, hell, I don't even do prescription drugs, it still hurts. I still shed a tear from time to time thinking about it. I'm ashamed, I'm sorry and I forgive myself now and forever.

But you know what, that was then and this is now. I'm back, sharper than ever, still gotta little swag and ready to serve. I feel good. It's only, only because God showed me favor and spared me that I come before you today on a mission to share my story in hopes that you may get a glimpse into and glean from it what you need.

We've all heard the saying there's no greater teacher like experience and I believe that, but, you know what, we can all learn so much from each other, would you agree? I sincerely pray that you get something of value out of this encounter with me..

WHY

Have you ever asked yourself why you were doing something? Ever asked yourself why me, why now, why this or why that? When I asked myself why I wanted to write this book and share my story, it became crystal clear as to why. Listen, if you've ever considered using drugs, and that includes all forms of alcohol as well as cigarettes I'm telling you, DON'T do it. If you're currently doing any form of drugs and you're wondering if you can quit I'm telling you, YES, you can. If you need help, I'm telling you, GET it now. If you're wondering if it's worth it, I'm telling you, Hell Yeah. If you've ever wondered if anyone loves you, I'm telling you, I LOVE YOU and that's WHY I'm writing this book.

I wrote this book because it's part of my destiny. You're reading it because it's part of yours. Now that destiny has joined us at the heart, let's make a positive and lasting impact on the world. Together. When destiny calls you answer. Now, you know why.

....

Why, because I said so.

....

Prayer

You can never underestimate the power of prayer. It worked in the past, it's working now and it will work in the future; however, only for those who believe. There are simply too many examples that prove the point. In my case, I prayed to be delivered from the grips of drug and alcohol abuse, and, as is customary, the creator answered the call. It's funny, at some point there was a certain feeling of calm and confidence that I would overcome the addiction. The really crazy part is, after I knew with certainty that I was going to quit, I had to get high one more time, one more for the road. I went on a seven-day binge where I got as high as I could on multiple forms of drugs, drank plenty of beer and prayed. It was the strangest thing. In the midst of the binge, I just kept praying and praying. On day number seven, I went cold turkey and haven't been high ever since. No drugs or alcohol for over 24 years...Hell, I don't even take prescription drugs. I can testify that PRAYER truly works.

The Bentley

My life is almost unrecognizable now...I'm an international best-selling author. I am a dynamic, charismatic, highly paid speaker and coach. Impacting the lives of those I speak to and coach in a positive manner that leads to transformation is what I do and I want to do that for you as well. It's so cool that I get to dress up in tailor made suits, custom made shirts with the finest accessories when presenting. I eat at fabulous restaurants, sleep in five-star beautiful hotels and rub elbows with industry giants as we perfect our craft. It's a beautiful thing. I'm coming to a town near you so stayed tuned. It's been a long time coming but finally, I'm playing full out on a first class all-star level. I am the best version of myself and I will never settle for mediocrity again. That's why I drive a Bentley Continental Flying Spur. To remind myself that I'm worthy of the best, always and forever. But make no mistake, this book isn't about a Bentley. I know it's a nice catchy title and I love it. It's not about my lifestyle, what I have and what I do. That's just stuff and stuff comes and goes. This book is about going from nothing to something, from drug addicted to drug free, from ordinary to extraordinary, from the bottom to the top, from the outhouse to the penthouse, from average to world class. This book is about not letting your beginning define you ending. What this book is truly about is continuously growing and evolving into the best human being I can be. Yes, this book is about the journey and the process. In order to have something you've never had, you have to become someone you've never been. And that's the magic, the secret sauce, it's about who you become. In short, it's not about what you have but WHO you are and I'm a Bentley kind of dude. I'm just saying.

....

I was badass at 22. I was badass at 32. I was badass at 42. I was badass at 52. I waited until 62 to show the world just how badass I am. Sorry for the delay.

....

East Lake

The Lake, as some of us call it, is a special place for me and crucial in my development. After all, I spent 10 years of my life there. For those of you who don't know, ELGC is where the last major golf tournament of the year is held. It's actually 2 tournaments in one. The Fed X Cup, which is the accumulative points leader for the year, and the Tour Championship. One player can actually win both and take home all the money which usually ranges around $10 to $13 million. Not bad for 4 days of work. You have the top 30 golfers in the world so it's kind of a big deal to say the least. Over the years, I've had personal conversations with a lot of them from Tiger Woods, Phil Mickelson, Jason Day, Jason Dufner, Dustin Johnson and many more. I've personally served Tiger his breakfast where I had a chance to converse with him. He's a cool guy and was very gracious to me. It's true, when Tiger walks in the room everything changes. One year, I was lucky enough to work in the players' locker room where I was up close and personal with these guys. That's when you learn they're just regular guys. They like cheese burgers, chicken wings, a ham sandwich and a beer like most other guys. Also, it's really cool to be in the room for the awards ceremony, you know, where select VIPs only get to be. Yes baby, I'm a VIP. It's different than what you see on TV. This tournament brings out the best and the worst of the staff every year. Though the tournament itself is only 4 days, Thursday-Sunday, it represents a couple of weeks of intense work for the staff inside and literally months for the grounds crew. We love to see it come and love to see it go. That's a once in a year thing but everyday something is happening at "The Lake"... There are all sorts of fundraisers and celebrity golf tournaments throughout the year. I've met everyone from Bo Jackson to Dr J, Roger Clemons, George "Iceman" Gervin, Matt Ryan, Warrick Dunn, Charles Barkley (thanks for the $100 tip), Larry Fitzgerald, Sterling Sharp, Greg Anderson, Ray Allen, LaDanian Thomlinson, Colts owner Robert Irsay (thanks for the $400 tip), Clyde Drexler, actors Anthony Anderson, Bill Murray, skier Lindsey Vonn (while dating Tiger) and the list goes on and on.

If you're ever fortunate enough to get there, you have to have some of Miss Dot's world famous potato salad. ELGC is special and not everyone gets to experience this ultra-private club regardless of how much money they have. Some of the members are legendary, mega wealthy and powerful in their own right. I learned a lot there, mostly about myself. Most notably, that, I'm badass too, I'm world class too. The last I checked, these guys put their pants on just like me. I asked a lot of questions while interacting with everyone I could and through that and great observation what became abundantly clear was these gentleman were simply living their life's dream, doing what they were called to do, simply living their life with a purpose on purpose. Then the light bulb came on...Jamaal, you've been shown all of this as a message, as a sign to move you to live your life's purpose as well. Thanks Universe.

To all the everyday members I had a chance to interact with and serve, you added value to my experience and motivated me to see what's possible. Marc Taylor, the "baddest" Attorney in Atlanta, I love you bro. We are forever joined at the hip and the heart.

To all my colleagues at ELGC, I want you to know you played a very special part in the growth and development of my life. Seriously, I am indebted to you all. After listening to you all bitch, moan and complain about everything yet about nothing all day every day, you confirmed to me that there's got to be more to life than this. (smile) I learned so much about myself observing you all and I really mean that in a positive way. ELGC may have been the best 10 years of my life from a development standpoint; it gave me what I needed when I needed it. I will never forget the times we had together. The laughs, the frustration, sneaking food from the buffet, arguing with that crazy Chef named Kevin, hiding from Chef Nick, the non-stop gossip and the love and support we showed for each other in the trenches. When the game started, we performed. It was organized chaos but we always got it done. There's only one "A TEAM" and we're it. I hope that I was able to leave your lives better as a result of knowing me. I'm your brother and y'all know I'm the best #4 and the world renowned best Bev-Cart GIRL EVER...It's too many of you all to mention by name other than Miss Dot since she's running the place anyway. Tell Mr. Rick I said hi. I love you all. It is my hope that this book inspires you to live life to the fullest...See y'all on 18

....

"Don't cry because it's over, smile because it happened." Dr. Seuss

....

The Wizard

If you love movies, you gotta love The Wizard of Oz. In my opinion, it's one of the greatest movies of all time. So many stories within the story. So many morals, values and principles acted out. If you want to see the Wizard, you follow the yellow brick road. Life is full of yellow brick roads that lead to whatever wizard you are pursuing. In this case, the wizard is nothing more than the end result of your labor, your desire, your ultimate goal in life. The yellow brick road represents certain, specific steps you need to take in order to get there. It represents consistency, it represents commitment as well as an unwavering faith and never stopping until you get there. But what if I told you the yellow brick road has shortcuts? Yes, only if Dorothy and the crew knew the yellow brick roads had shortcuts, they could have shortened their trip. The shortcut to success is coaching. Coaching, what do you mean Jamaal? Well, let me answer it with these real world examples...The great MLK had two particular coaches that had a tremendous impact on his life and it's funny how you very seldom, if ever, hear about that. But these two were instrumental in his development and success. Oprah Winfrey is reported to have, get this, seven coaches, one for every important area of her life. If this concept and strategy is good enough for Oprah, surely it's good enough for you. Tiger Woods, one of the greatest golfers the world has ever seen, has a coach. He has a putting coach, a swing coach, a financial coach, heck, he even has a media coach. Notice how polished he always sounds in his interviews? Did you know that every serious golfer on tour has a coach? All major tennis players have a coach. This powerful strategy is not just limited to athletes. Check this out.

Warren Buffet, arguably the best investor the world has ever seen or known, was heavily influenced by his Columbia University Professor Benjamin Graham, whom he later went on to work for at Grahams brokerage firm. Though their philosophies differed somewhat, the foundation for Buffet's massive success started with Benjamin Graham. Bill Gates has many coaches, Warren Buffet being one of them. Gates and co-founder Paul Allen had Ed Roberts early in their careers. In fact, it was Ed Roberts who let these two unknowns test their unproven software on HIS computer which led to them starting Microsoft. Steve Jobs, one of the 3 founders of Apple computers, also had many coaches with Andy Grove being the most influential. Albert Einstein had Max Talmey. Henry Ford had Thomas Edison.

Thomas Edison had Franklin Leonard Pope. Winston Churchill had Bourke Cochran. Benjamin Franklin had James Logan. Samuel Clemens, better known as Mark Twain, had Artemus Ward. The great Hellen Keller had "the miracle lady" Anne Sullivan. Alexander the Great had

Aristotle. Aristotle had Plato, Plato had Socrates.

It is said that the shortest distance between two points is a straight line. Coaching is that straight line. My man, Tony Robbins, made the term "modeling" popular. You simply "model" the activities of your coach. Another way to put it is you "copy" your coach's every move. Put yet another way, and a term I know you're familiar with is "don't reinvent the wheel". Why would you want to do that when the wheel is working perfectly? Make it easy on yourself, achieve what you want in life quicker by getting expert coaching, by copying, by modeling, by following the yellow brick road.

Remember, the Scarecrow, the Cowardly Lion and the Tin Man, they already had what they needed inside of them. Hell, even Dorothy just had to close her eyes and click her heels three times and she was back at home in Kansas. What is Kansas for you, where is Kansas for you, are you willing to do what you're told like Dorothy to get to where you want to go? All too often, what many of us really need is a little push, a little guidance, a little love, and depending on who we are a little or a lot of coaching. Coaching is a powerful tool that cuts years off your learning curve, alleviate undue pain, stress and usually saves the student a lot of money.

Coaching is a powerful tool, use it. I often wonder, what if understood and applied these 30 years ago? How many years can you afford to give away?

Do you want to be great now or later? If not now, WHEN?

Yesterday is gone forever, tomorrow will not come for many so understand clearly that NOW is all you have. Your life is NOW. You're gazing into your future now. You're looking back at your past now. Whatever you're gonna make of yourself, you have to do it now.

Very few of us are fortunate enough to be like a Michael Jackson or a Shirley Temple where we get to live the vast majority, if not all of our life, on top doing the thing we love to do. Harlan Sanders better known as Colonel Sanders was just an average guy until he finally put it all together and founded Kentucky Fried Chicken at age 65. What if he had started at 25? That's 40 more years of being the King of Chicken...Celebrity Chef Julia Child did not write her first cook book until age 50... Samuel L Jackson's career didn't take off until age 48 in the film Jungle Fever...Henry Ford was 45 when he created the legendary Model T...Rodney Dangerfield didn't catch a break until "The Ed Sullivan Show" at age 46...In 1954 at age 52, Ray Kroc bought McDonalds and the rest is history. Don't wait to be great. Don't wait to live your purpose...Whatever you do, don't wait. Someone in the world is looking for you, right now.

When I became clear and decided I wanted to speak from the stage for a living, the universe started working on my behalf as it always does. A chance encounter with the legendary Les Brown sealed the deal. I had been watching his videos for quite some time when I met him while working. After a five-minute conversation with him, instead of wanting to be like Mike, I wanted to be like Les.

Guess what, now, he's one of my coaches. It's so cool and it's no coincidence that our paths crossed. There is a saying that, "What you are seeking is seeking you"...Les was seeking students and I was seeking a teacher...To know what I know and do what I do now would never have been possible without the expert guidance and coaching from Les Brown. Of course, Les Brown himself has a coach. His name is Mike Williams, a successful coach to many. In fact, Les shares the story of how it was Mike Williams who encouraged him to start speaking while he was still a successful celebrity DJ in Miami. Les said he never saw that for himself, and since he was comfortable being a DJ, he never would have chosen to be a speaker.

As fate would have it, he got fired as a DJ and that's when he took this speaking thing seriously. Now, Les is considered by many to be the #1 motivational speaker in the world. I'm telling you all the great ones have a coach and some multiple coaches. If you want to be mediocre, if you want to be average, if you want to play it small, if you want to continue to live paycheck to paycheck then continue to go it alone. It's okay, there's plenty of room in the middle. But if you want to be great, if you want to be world class, if you want to live your dreams, if you want to make a difference in the lives of many then get yourself a coach, period, end of story.

....

If you want to go fast go alone. If you want to go far go together.
African proverb

....

Purpose

Who am I, why am I here, and where am I going? Have you ever asked yourself these questions? These are very powerful questions that need serious introspection. Can I tell you something that's worse than death? I know you're like come on Jamaal what can be worse than death. I'll tell you what, a life without purpose is worse than death. To live fifty, sixty, seventy or even eighty years and never know why, is a tragedy. After 80 years, you still don't know who you are, why you're here and where you're going. After 80 years, you never figured it out, that's 80 years wasted. Without a purpose, life has no meaning, no sense of destiny. There are over 7 billion people on the planet, and contrary to some opinions, not one of us is a mistake. Each one of us was sent here to do something that has value for the rest of us. In other words. God needed something to be done that made you necessary.

Everything and everyone has a purpose, but most of us have no idea what our purpose is. We are obligated to find out. Let me say this, there is no substitute for purpose. If you are trying to become something that you are not then you are abusing who you are. I repeat, there is no substitute for purpose. You cannot turn a car into a boat or a boat into a plane. Finding your purpose is the most important discovery you can make. Napoleon Hill in his best-selling timeless classic, "Think and Grow Rich" says that "desire" is the starting point of all achievement. That desire leads to your purpose.

You can do anything, but not everything. Find that ONE thing that only you can do and do it until you can't do it anymore.

You have a divine assignment that you must fulfill. Until you discover your personal reason for living, you will never be fulfilled. Put another way, until you discover your purpose, you can never maximize your potential. If you never maximize your potential, you're cheating and it becomes the ultimate act of ingratitude. Being ungrateful is so not cool. Dr. Myles Munroe puts it this way, he says, "If you did everything everybody wanted you to do but not what you were born to do then what you were born to do will haunt what you did." You know some people who on the outside look to be successful. They have the prestigious career titles of a doctor, lawyer, university professor or a businessman but they are miserable as hell because all the while what they really want to do is be on American Idol and pursue their love for music, paint portraits or start their own restaurant. Too many are doctors because that's what their doctor mother and father wanted them to be. Life is too short and too valuable to live someone else's dream. You'll never see an eagle trying to be a chicken. The fish knows to stay in the water. Yes, its skillset is designed to be in the water and because it knows this and is obedient to its nature, it flourishes, it thrives, and there it is fulfilled.

Who's ever heard of a guy by the name of Michael Jackson? Would it be safe to say that Michael Jackson was not only abundantly clear but he was definitely definite about his purpose in life? Now, to be fair, very few of us are that clear that early in life about what our purpose as MJ was but he certainly is not an exception to the rule and our lives are all the better because of it. He touched millions upon millions of people around the globe because he lived his purpose.

But you see, if Michael Jackson had decided he wanted to be Michael Jordan, he would have never become Michael Jackson. He would have missed his blessing, his calling, his divine assignment and his purpose and so would we.

They call him the king, and by the trajectory of his career, they might be right.

LeBron James was born to play Basketball. He was also a high school football star. I'm sure if he wanted to be a rapper, a historian or an engineer, based on who he is, he would have succeeded at it. But, LeBron James was born to play Basketball, and again, I say the world has been blessed to witness his talent all because he identified and committed to living his purpose.

Did you know that Sammy Davis Junior's mother and

father were also vaudeville singers and dancers and young Sammy first appeared onstage at age 3 becoming a regular at age 5? Do you think the fact that his mom and dad were vaudeville singers and dancers had anything to do with Sammy becoming a vaudeville singer and dancer? It's clear to me this was Sammy's purpose for he crushed it.

Who's old enough to remember Shirley Temple? When I was a young lad and watching her on TV, I used to say to myself, "How can she do that, act with that kind of command, that kind of control, that kind of confidence? At the time, I had no idea of the concept and of the value of definiteness of purpose. Now, since I've grown a little and matured, I understand that's the only way she could have done it. She was simply living her purpose, and boy, did it show.

Les Brown, my friend and mentor is considered by many to be the world's best motivational speaker. Now, Les has done a lot of things. He was a successful DJ in Miami, a very impactful junior senator in the Ohio legislature, and, you got to be pretty sharp to marry one of the legendary singers of all time in Gladys Night of the Pips. No, that's not a small feat. But Les' crown achievement in life is being a speaker. Check this out, Les is so good that he makes more money in one hour than most Americans make in one year. Let's put this in perspective. The average working week for most Americans, 40 hours, multiplied by 52 weeks is 2080 hours. You mean to tell me that you can be so good at what you do that you can command in one hour what it takes most folks 2080 hours to do? C'mon, is that even fair? On the surface, one would say no way. What If I told you that Les Brown worked 2080 hours upfront perfecting his craft before he ever made a dime? Les worked on himself, worked on his belief, and learned hundreds of quotes; he practiced until he became the Les Brown that commands a year's salary in one hour. It's fair because Mrs. Mammie Brown's baby boy is living his purpose, therefore adding tremendous value to the market place, and the more value you bring to the market place the more it pays you. Les, and others like him, get exactly what they deserve. The average worker in America gets what they deserve as well. I know it sounds cold but it's true. No disrespect to the dishwasher, the waiter or the cook, the cashier at Walmart or the Lyft and Uber driver. It's just that you can find that kind of talent anywhere, all day every day, give them 2 hours' worth of training and turn them loose. Because they bring very little value to the market place, they get paid very little. To be perfectly honest, this is the purpose for some people working in those areas. Some people are going to be waiters and cooks all their life and they are damn good at it. You can tell these waiters apart from the rest because they are passionate about serving you versus someone who is just in it for a paycheck to make ends meet. I hope I didn't offend anyone and I hope it's a point well taken. Just so you know, I've waited tables, bussed tables, been a short order cook, and driven for Lyft and Uber.

We can go on and on with example after example of people who chose to live their life with passion on purpose. The childhood stars I mentioned above are certainly not the norm. I think we all would agree that the norm is people like you and I. People who had already lived most of their lifetime before they figured it out. I also proved with some earlier examples that it's never too late to get started. As long as there is still time on the clock, you have an opportunity to win. Besides, as Les Brown says, "It ain't over until I win".

....

Take up one idea. Make that one idea your life — think of it, dream of it, and live on that idea. Let the brain, muscles, nerves, and every other part of your body, be full of that idea, and just leave every other idea alone. This is the way to success. ~Swami Vivekananda

....

Regret

Some years ago, there was a study done with 100 people who were at the end of their life and they were asked the question, what do you regret most about your life. Interesting enough, not one of them spoke of what they did or had done, they all spoke of what they didn't do, the pain of regret for NOT DOING what's number one on the list. The books never written, the recipes never perfected, the businesses never started, the degrees never finished, the vacations never taken and countries never visited. Many of the women reported regretting never getting married and having children. Don't let this be you, but if you're not careful it could be you. Time is constantly moving and it waits for no one. Get busy so you'll never have to say I coulda woulda shoulda..

Again, I want to share with you a little about the story of Colonel Sanders. I love it, there is so much to learn from it. Here's a man that started one of the most iconic restaurant franchises of all time and he didn't do it until age 65. Amazing.

While most people his age were busy riding off into

the Florida sunset, he was busy pursuing his passion to give the world his unique chicken recipe. Because he persisted, because he persevered, because he kept his dream alive, there are more than 14,000 KFCs in more than 100 countries. If this is not a great, inspiring example of what passion, purpose and dreams are about then I don't know what is.

But what if, what if he had started at 25 instead of 65? That's 40 more years of being the "chicken king"...Just think how much more impact he could have had, how many more lives he could have touched, influenced and inspired. I'm just saying, there are things you'll do at 25, 35 and 45 you won't at 65. Still, his story is a beautiful one. Remember, once time has passed you can never get it back.

My mentor Les Brown shared with me how he procrastinated for 8 to 10 years before he actually started doing what he needed to do to become the legendary speaker we all know. He spoke of going to all the seminars and conferences of the greats and not so greats and saying to himself I can do that. I can do that. But he didn't do that. He let fear and all its friends and relatives convince him that he couldn't. He found every excuse in the book to not pursue his gift of speaking. Thank the Universe that he found the courage to stand up and be counted, to stand up and deliver as only he can do.

Once you declare that you want to do a thing, it seems all kind of forces come out of nowhere to tell you can't do it. But I'm here to tell you, press on my friend because once these forces realize that you will not be denied they step aside and let you pass through...And even they quietly applaud your tenacity and hunger to succeed. Les Brown was hungry.

Besides, what's on the other end of not living your dream? If you don't know already let me tell you, it's not good. It's called mediocrity. It's called living from paycheck to paycheck...The O'jays had a popular song in the seventies called "living for the weekend"...Are you serious, the weekend is all you live for? This is real talk and far too many people fall into this category. I think the label is called the masses. Are you in this group? If so, do you want to get out? You see, the people in this group find it hard to go on vacation when they want if they go at all. Many people in this group are stuck with when they have the time they don't have the money and when they have the money they don't have the time. Can you imagine not being able to go to a close relative's funeral because you don't have the time or money? That's insane yet it happens all the time. Do you constantly miss your son or daughter's events at school because you can't get off work? Have you ever seen cars running around with tapped plastic on the windows or obvious damage from accidents? They can't afford to get a new window or get the car repaired because they live from paycheck to paycheck and there's no extra money for stuff like that. Yet they work every day every week and have been for years. Did you know the average American has less than $500 in their saving account? Bankrate.com reported in 2012 that 28 percent of American families have no savings. Another 20 percent don't have enough saved to cover even three months' worth of living expenses, while just 43 percent have enough in savings to cover three months of expenses. It's pretty sad. There is a serious price to pay for being world class, being on top, living your purpose and controlling your own destiny. But I submit to you my dear friend that the price of mediocrity, of being average and controlled by someone else is a far greater price to pay. Been there, done that. Listen, you're gonna pay the price either way, why not choose to truly live instead of just existing...The pain of regret is real.

The late great Myles Munroe said the wealthiest place on the planet is not in the Far East where there's oil in the ground or South Africa where there are Diamond mines, he said the wealthiest place on the planet is the cemetery because there you'll find potential never realized, dreams never pursued, there, you'll find people who allowed themselves to be imprisoned by fear who lived a small life.

It was Henry David Thoreau who said, "Oh God, to reach the point of death only to realize you've never lived, only to realize you've never scrapped the surface of your potential". Wow, that's too deep. Don't let this be you, live your life in a big way for the benefit of everyone. You make the world a better place when you live your life in a dynamic, powerful way that's geared towards serving others. Yes, the world needs you to play big. Time out for average.

Let me submit to you that average is over. We're in a time in our existence, in our evolution as a society that you're either going to excel or be left out. Not left behind but left out. With over seven billion people on the planet, you want to get in the game, excellence is required, you want to get in the game, greatness is required, and to stay in the game you need to be at the top of your game. Nowadays, when you apply for a position in the workplace, the competition is stiff, to say the least. You may have 500, 1000, 1500 or more applicants in front of you. Now, the employer has the luxury to discriminate and pick the cream of the crop. If there is such a thing as good discrimination, this would be it as only the best will do. That's just the way it is. The world demands greatness and you have it. Average is a dime for five dozen these days. Yes, the world has changed, competition is at an all-time high and not slowing down anytime soon. You have a choice to make and sense "average" is not an option, I'll see you at the top.

> "I remembered that throughout my growing up and my education and pursuing my dreams and desires, going into action, and, of course getting through Yale University and on and on and on, that being average, that being mediocre was not an option that I would be proud of." **Angela Bassett**

> "Playing athletics, playing a lot of different sports, going into drama school…I was one of those kids who wanted to do everything, so I ended up being pretty average at everything." **Matt Bomer**

> "You don't win Championships by just being normal, by just being average." **Bill Walton**

"I'm intimidated by the fear of being average." **Taylor Swift**

"The average is the borderline that keeps mere men in their place. Those who step over the line are heroes by the very act. Go." **Henry Rollins**

"The hell with average, be awesome or be forgotten." **Jamaal Ali**

Would you trust your life to an "average" surgeon? Would you have an "average" attorney on retainer to protect your property or reputation? Would you want an "average" accountant to handle your finances? Of course not, because when it comes to important things "average" is not an acceptable standard for comparison. Don't be average, go above and beyond and adopt a higher standard.

....

On average, it takes 35 hours to build a Toyota. On average, it takes 105 days to build a Rolls Royce

....

The Sweet Spot

Jackie Gleason, that hilarious and talented actor used to say in the Honey Mooners TV series, "How sweet it is. He was one of my favorite actors and I loved hearing him say that. He said it in such a way that you knew life was sweet for him. And truly, life is sweet when you know who you are, why you're here and where you're going. When you're in that sweet spot or the zone, where nothing else seems to matter, when time stands still, yes, when you're in that space you know you're living your purpose. But the million dollar question is, how do we get there? Aww, I thought you'd never ask. I want to leave you with some tools and strategies that if taken seriously and applied can help you find yourself and start living your life's purpose. And keep in mind, there is no one way to do this, not everything works for everyone, there are many different approaches but all are very similar. But first things first.

It is my humble opinion that finding your purpose in life is the most important thing you can do.

Here's a story about Bruce Lee which sets the stage for the exercises that will follow. A master martial artist asked Bruce to teach him everything Bruce knew about martial arts. Bruce held up two cups, both filled with liquid. "The first cup," said Bruce, "represents all of your knowledge about martial arts. The second cup represents all of my knowledge about martial arts. If you want to fill your cup with my knowledge, you must first empty your cup of your knowledge."

When you saw Bruce Lee perform not only did you see perfection, you saw purpose in motion. Indeed, Bruce was one of a kind. But so are you, we all are. As long as you stay in the pack, in the herd, in the middle no one will ever know. Get out.

If you want to discover your true purpose in life, you must first empty your mind of all the false purposes you've been taught, all the preconceived notions and ideas that have led you to where you are. Here is a very simple barometer to use. If you're not happy doing what you're doing, that's a strong proof that you're not living your purpose.

Understand that this is going to involve some work. Some work you've most likely never done so be willing to work and be open to the process. I want to caution you here. Even though the work required here is simple, don't let the simplicity fool you. It's seems it's human nature to devalue processes when they are simple. Somewhere at some point in time it seems we were taught that for things to be legitimate and effective, they have to be hard? Erase that nonsense now.

You are going to have to write, if you don't like

writing, get over it. You can either do it the old-fashioned way and take pen and paper or you can write using your computer. Your choice. Be honest, this is your private time with yourself, no one will read it but you. Enjoy the moment and make it fun. Ready, here goes.

1. Find a place where you will not be interrupted. Turn off your cell phone, the TV and anything that might distract you.
2. Begin by listing all the things that are most important to you. Your values, your morals and your goals. Reflect on these because they will be in alignment with your purpose.
3. Make a list of questions to ask yourself that will jog your memory and get your juices flowing and I think the next question is a great place to start.
4. If money wasn't an issue, what would I do every day all day for the rest of my life?
5. What is that one thing that excited you most as a kid?
6. What makes you smile, makes you feel good, makes you laugh? as in activities, people, events, hobbies, projects, etc.
7. What activities make you lose track of time?
8. What are you naturally good at? Painting, singing, cooking etc.
9. What do others say you're good at? Sometimes what others see in you is a great clue to the real you.
10. What is or was your favorite pastime?
11. If you could teach something, what would you teach?

12. Who are your favorite teachers? Not only what they teach, but how and who they are and why you're attracted to them could be revealing.
13. What do you like most about yourself?
14. What would you regret not doing, being or having in your life?
15. You only get to do one thing in life, what is it?
16. What causes do you strongly connect with and believe in?
17. It's your 90th birthday, the kids and grandkids have taken you to the beach. As they go off in different directions and you have a moment of silence to reflect on your life, what would matter most?
18. This may be a little creepy to some but helps put things into perspective. Besides, it's real life. The day has finally come and you are laid to rest. Yes, it's your funeral. What will they say about you? What would you want them to say about you? After it's said and done, how would you want to be remembered? What is your legacy? This is you last time to get it right...(smile)

Write the answers to each of your questions down. Write the first thing that pops into your mind. Don't overthink, don't force it. It's critically important to write out your answers rather than just thinking about them. There is magic in writing them down, they come to life that way.

This is a great list to get you started and may be all you need. Add as many questions as is necessary to find your purpose. Write for as long as you need to. This is serious business, this is your life.

Also, a very important exercise to incorporate into the mix is Your Personal Mission Statement.

"Writing or reviewing a mission statement changes you because it forces you to think through your priorities deeply, carefully, and to align your behavior with your beliefs."

~**Stephen Covey,** '7 *Habits of Highly Effective People*'

A personal mission consists of 3 parts:

What do I want to do?

Who do I want to help?

What is the result? What value will I create?

5 quick Steps to Creating Your Personal Mission Statement:

1. Do the exercise with the 15 questions above as quickly as you can.
2. List out some of the action words you connect with.

a. For instance: educate, accomplish, empower, encourage, improve, help, give, guide, inspire, integrate, master, motivate, nurture, organize, produce, promote, travel, spread, share, satisfy, understand, teach, write, etc.

3. Based on your answers to the 15 questions. List everything and everyone that you believe you can help.

a. As in: People, creatures, organizations, causes, groups, environment, etc.

4. Identify your end goal. How will the 'who' from your above answer benefit from what you 'do'?
5. Combine steps 2-4 into a sentence, or 2-3 sentences, if necessary, but the more concise, the

better. After this you should have a clear mission statement and clear purpose for your life.

Congratulations...I commend you for choosing to live life to the fullest, to live life with intention and purpose, to live big, to live.

....

The whole secret to a successful life is to find out what is one's destiny to do, and then do it...Henry Ford

....

Going Inside

I'm simply saying that there is a way to be sane. I'm saying that you can get rid of all this insanity created by the past in you. Just by being a simple witness of your thought processes. It is simply sitting silently, witnessing the thoughts, passing before you. Just witnessing, not interfering not even judging, because the moment you judge you have lost the pure witness. The moment you say "this is good, this is bad," you have already jumped onto the thought process.

It takes a little time to create a gap between the witness and the mind. Once the gap is there, you are in for a great surprise, that you are not the mind, that you are the witness, a watcher. And this process of watching is the very alchemy of real religion. Because as you become more and more deeply rooted in witnessing, thoughts start disappearing. You are, but the mind is utterly empty. That's the moment of enlightenment. That is the moment that you become for the first time an unconditioned, sane, really free human being.

In today's world, sitting down, quieting the mind,

relaxing, breathing deeply and being in the moment is utterly impossible. And no, you can't create an app for the ancient art and application of simple meditation. Well, it's utterly impossible for most people, the masses, the average, the everyday Joe and Jane.

Question, could this be one of the reasons they are in this category? It's highly likely AND here's why I say that. Success is a result of our daily habits and so is failure. The vast majority of successful people meditate on a daily basis, you know, like every day. Why, well, because they studied other successful people and they found that's what successful people do, and wanting to be successful themselves, they incorporated meditation into their daily activity and it helped them become successful. That's kind of like a riddle but you get the point. If not let me make it clear. Meditation is critical to your success. You see, in order to get out you have to go in. The masses of people are living life inside out upside down and backwards. That's why there's a ball of confusion out there. Forget about the world, get in order with yourself and your world will be in order. If you want a more powerful, dynamic and stress free life, meditate. If you want more clarity and direction, meditate. In short, if you want a fuller expression of your life, then meditate daily.

There are numerous books, videos and classes on meditation for you to learn this marvelous life changing technique. Remember we talked about living your purpose. Well, mastering and teaching meditation is the purpose of many people, seek them out, they are looking for you.

How you start your day is the key to your day, it sets the tone for and shapes your day. Start your day with meditation. End your day with meditation, and if you can find 6 or 7 minutes during the day to meditate, try to. Meditation opens you up for that all important paradigm shift to take place. As Jim Rhon says, "in order for things to change you have to change". Everyone wants to change the world but no one wants to change themselves. Nope, it doesn't work like that. Understand, when you change yourself you change the world. All change starts within.

....

Beautify your inner dialogue. Beautify your inner world with love, light and compassion. Your life will be beautiful...Amit Ray

....

Daily Affirmation by Dr Joseph Murphy

I know there is only one source, the life principal, the living spirit from which all things flow. It created the Universe and all things therein contained. I am a focal point of Divine presence. My mind is open and receptive. I am a free-flowing channel for harmony, beauty, guidance, wealth and the riches of the infinite. I know that wealth, health and success are released from within and appear on the without. I am now in harmony with the infinite riches within and without, and I know these thoughts are sinking into my subconscious mind, and will be reflected on the screen of space. I wish for everyone all the blessings of life. I am open and receptive to the Divine riches, spiritual, mental and material, and they flow to me in avalanches of abundance.

P.S. Recite 5 minutes before bed and the first 5 minutes after waking.

You and I

Life is beautiful, with all the ups and downs, ins and outs, all the hills and valleys and everything in between. You wouldn't know what the taste of sweet is without tasting something bitter. In order to enjoy the pleasure, you have to stand the pain. Remember, the beautiful flowers and greenery that you see all around need the rain to blossom...So stop complaining when it rains. Embrace it and learn to love the rain. Rain is a beautiful thing that brings with it many blessings. It is my hope that I have shared something of myself that proves to be valuable to you. However, only so much can be shared in a book and this wonderful connection we now have must continue. I insist. Besides, I want to learn from you too. That's why I'm inviting you to connect with me via my website at www.jamaalali.com so that I may further serve you. Or visit me on social media via Facebook at
www.facebook.com/transform20three where we can interact. I look forward to meeting you.
Peace and Prosperity,

Jamaal

www.ingramcontent.com/pod-product-compliance
Lightning Source LLC
Chambersburg PA
CBHW070043260726
48658CB00002B/711